Gorillas in the wild

Cliff Moon

Wayland

In the Wild

Alligators and Crocodiles in the wild
Elephants in the wild
Giraffes in the wild
Gorillas in the wild
Kangaroos in the wild
Lions in the wild
Pandas in the wild
Penguins in the wild
Tigers in the wild
Whales and Dolphins in the wild

This book is based on an original text by Anthony Wootton

First published in 1984 by
Wayland (Publishers) Ltd
49 Lansdowne Place, Hove
East Sussex BN3 1HF, England

ISBN 0 85078 443 3

Phototypeset by
Kalligraphics Ltd, Redhill, Surrey
Printed in Italy by
G. Canale & C.S.p.A., Turin
Bound in the UK by
The Pitman Press, Bath

Contents

To Sam
Im so
sorry your
leaving but
think of me
by the
book
Love
Lizzygold.
xxxxxxxxxxxxxx

Gorillas

Have you ever seen a gorilla?
Zoos have to keep gorillas in cages
because they are so big and strong.

But wild gorillas live together
in family groups and
they move about all the time.
The gorillas you see in zoos
often look sad because
they have to stay in their cages.

This is a fully grown gorilla.
It weighs the same as
three adult people.
It looks very fierce but
it is quite friendly really.

This is an adult Mountain gorilla.
Mountain gorillas live in forests
on the mountain slopes of Rwanda.
They have longer, silkier hair
than other gorillas and
they are hard to find
because there aren't many left.

This adult male gorilla
is a very powerful animal.
People used to think that
gorillas would attack them but
they will only fight
if someone harms them.

Gorillas have long forearms
and short back legs.
They have massive shoulders.

Gorillas have very strong jaws
and sharp teeth.
They can see, hear and smell
better than most animals.

Here is a **silverback** male gorilla.
He is called a silverback
because he has silver hair
all down his back.
Gorillas live in family groups and
the silverback is the leader.

Male gorillas are taller and heavier than females.
When a fully grown male stands up he can be 2 metres (over 6 ft) tall and he can weigh up to 300 kg (650 lbs).

Gorillas walk on all fours
most of the time but
sometimes they stand up.

Do you think gorillas
move quickly or slowly?
(Answer on page 58)

This **zoologist** is studying gorillas.
The gorilla will not attack him
if he moves slowly and
makes sure he can be seen
all the time.
The gorilla is roaring loudly.
It is telling the zoologist
not to come any nearer.

Gorillas live in Central Africa
where there are forests, lakes and rivers.
It is always hot and wet
in the thick African forests.

We know that gorillas
have lived in that part of Africa
for thousands of years because
people have found their **fossils**
buried in the ground.

There are only three gorilla races:
Western Lowland gorillas,
Eastern Lowland gorillas
and Mountain gorillas.

At Home in the Wild

Many people think that gorillas spend their time climbing trees and swinging from branch to branch. But gorillas are very heavy. If a branch breaks they will crash to the ground. Sometimes female gorillas make nests in the trees for sleeping or feeding in.

This silverback gorilla is climbing a tree but he is too heavy to make a nest there. So where will he sleep?
(Answer on page 58)

Here is a silverback Mountain gorilla.

Between six and thirty gorillas
live in each family group.
Most of them are females with
their babies and young gorillas.
The silverback is their leader.

Gorillas eat fruit, roots,
leaves, bamboo shoots and tree bark.
They are fond of wild celery
and banana stems.
This gorilla is eating bamboo stems.

Female gorillas may build nests
of branches and leaves
about 6 metres (20 ft) up
in the trees.
If there are not many trees,
or if the trees are not
strong enough to hold them,
they build their nests on the ground.

The zoologist is watching
a family group.
The gorillas seldom fight or quarrel.
The silverback male is the biggest but
he does not bully the others.

This silverback male is roaring
because another family group
has come too close.
He beats his chest and
runs about to frighten
the other group away.

The roaring gorilla looks fierce
with his staring eyes and
big sharp teeth.
Do you think he will fight
the other group's silverback?
(Answer on page 58)

This Mountain gorilla is eating bark.

Here is a Mountain gorilla
asleep on a tree branch
in a National Park in Zaire.

These young Mountain gorillas
are playing a game.
They are chasing each other
up and down the tree.

Baby Gorillas

A female gorilla has her first baby
when she is 6 or 7 years old.
She mates with the male silverback
and her baby is born
about nine months later.
The baby weighs about 2 kg
(4 to 5 lb) when it is born but
it grows up much faster than
a human baby.
It can walk when it is
four months old and
it starts to climb trees
when it is six months old.

This baby gorilla is clinging
to its mother's hair
as she climbs down the steps
in a zoo.

This baby gorilla was born in a zoo.

A baby gorilla can feed itself
when it is one year old
but it stays with its mother
and drinks her milk
until it is three years old.

A mother gorilla **grooms** her baby.
She scratches and combs
her baby's hair – this shows
how much she cares for it.

Here is a mother gorilla
grooming her baby.

This gorilla enjoys eating leaves.

Young gorillas are very playful.
Sometimes they climb all over the male silverback, teasing him.
What do you think he does when he gets fed up?
(Answer on page 58)

About half of the babies
become ill and die before
they are fully grown.
When that happens the female
mates and has another baby.

Even in a zoo a young gorilla
will find something to play with.

This young gorilla is following
his father up a tree.
He will grow up to be a silverback too.
It will take 8 or 9 years
to become an adult male but
it takes even longer
to become a silverback.

This adult male is now a silverback.
But there is already a silverback
in his family group.
He may wander off and
join another group or
he may take over as leader
if the other silverback is getting old.

Staying Alive

Gorillas do not often get attacked
by other animals because
they are so big and strong.
Sometimes a young gorilla strays
from the family group and
gets killed by a leopard.

Many gorillas die because
they catch diseases and
that often happens to their babies.

There are only a few thousand
Mountain gorillas like this left.
Can you think why?
(Answer on page 59)

This Western Lowland gorilla
is safer than the Mountain gorillas.
There are still plenty of forests
where it can find food.

These gorillas are feeding
in a farmer's bean field.
If the farmer sees them
he may shoot them.

People used to catch gorillas
and kill them to show them off
to their friends.
That does not often happen now but
this baby Mountain gorilla
has no mother because
she has been killed.

Tribesmen like these used to kill
gorillas so that they could
cook the meat and eat it.
They also made medicine
from gorilla bones and brains.
Can you think why?
(Answer on page 59)

These gorillas are eating banana
stems and fruit.
They can ruin a farmer's crop
in a few hours.

One way to save gorillas
is to breed them in zoos but
gorillas like to be free and
they don't breed well in cages.

This gorilla can eat its bamboo
in the safety of the forest.

Another thing that happens in zoos
is that gorillas catch human diseases.
So they can sometimes die
just as easily in a zoo
as they can in the wild.

Gorillas often foul their nests
so they always build
new nests each night.
Even so, they pass diseases
to each other very easily
when they foul their nests.

Gorillas and Humans

The way a gorilla sits and looks reminds us of ourselves.

In 1859 Charles Darwin said that human beings and apes developed from the same animals millions of years ago. When you watch a gorilla it is easy to see why Charles Darwin said that.

Many people believe that Charles Darwin was right. Can you think why?
(Answer on page 59)

Most other apes, like monkeys, spend a lot of their time in trees but gorillas live quite happily on the ground most of the time.

This gorilla is roaring and
hooting to scare away other gorillas.
Gorillas can tell each other things
by the different noises they make.

These Mountain gorillas are lucky.
They live in a mountain forest
which isn't being cut down
to make new farmland.

People have tried to teach gorillas
to speak like humans but
they have given up.
Gorillas lead simple lives,
so they do not need to speak.

A gorilla can look just like
a human who is thinking
about something.

Gorillas can work out the best way
to solve a problem.
They cup their hands to catch
dripping water and they use sticks
to get at their food.

They take great care of each other
and when they are in a zoo,
they even take care of their keeper!

They are very fussy about their food.
They eat their favourite bits
and leave the rest,
just like humans.
What do you think they do
with the scraps when
they have finished eating?
(Answer on page 59)

What is this gorilla thinking?

Gorillas are interested in everything that happens around them. They watch carefully and think about what is going on.

One day some African workers were building a new road. A family of gorillas arrived, sat by the side of the road and watched the workers for over half an hour! No one knows why they watched and no one knows what they were thinking.

Answers to Questions

Page 17
Gorillas move quite slowly
but they can move faster
than people through thick jungle.

Page 21
The heavy silverback male gorilla
always sleeps on the ground.
No tree branch is strong enough
to bear his great weight.

Page 27
Male silverbacks look fierce but
they seldom fight each other.
They would rather give in
than have a fight.

Page 34
When the male silverback
gets fed up with the teasing
he smacks the young gorillas
on their bottoms!

Page 39
There are only a few thousand Mountain gorillas left because farmers are using the land where they live.

Page 43
Tribesmen used to make medicine from gorilla bones and brains because they believed it would make them strong and healthy.

Page 49
Many people believe that humans and apes developed from the same animals because the fossils of apes and early humans are very similar.

Page 54
When gorillas have finished eating they leave the scraps in neat, tidy piles.

Index

Picture Acknowledgements
Ardea/Kenneth Fink 32; Colour Library International 43; Bruce Coleman Limited by the following photographers: Lee Lyon endpapers 11, 14, 15, 20, 22, 23, 25, 26, 27, 28, 29, 33, 34, 36, 41, 44–5, 46, 51; Bruce Coleman 12, 35, 55; Norman Tomalin 16–17, 30, 48; G. D. Plage 18; Jospeh Van Wormer 35; R. M. Campbell 52–3; Sullivan and Rogers 40; George B. Schaller 47; Christian Zuber front cover; Jerry Cooke/Oxford Scientific Films Ltd/Animals Animals 8; Survival Anglia/Colin Willock 10, 13/Lee Lyon, 24, 37, 38, 42; Zefa/W. Lummer 56.